MW01118426

The Cherokee

by Petra Press

Content Adviser: Professor Sherry L. Field,
Department of Social Science Education, College of Education,
The University of Georgia

Reading Adviser: Dr. Linda D. Labbo,
Department of Reading Education, College of Education,
The University of Georgia

COMPASS POINT BOOKS

Minneapolis, Minnesota

FIRST REPORTS

Compass Point Books
3722 West 50th Street, #115
Minneapolis, MN 55410

Visit Compass Point Books on the Internet at *www.compasspointbooks.com* or e-mail your request
to *custserv@compasspointbooks.com*

Front cover: A Cherokee carrying basket from 1941

Photographs ©: The Philbrook Museum of Art, Tulsa, Oklahoma/Don Wheeler 1948.39.196
(Carrying basket, 1941, Nancy Bradley, Cherokee, Cane, Gift of Clark Field), cover; Unicorn
Stock Photos/Jean Higgins, 4; Sharon Gerig/Tom Stack and Associates, 5; XNR Productions, Inc.,
7; John Shaw/Tom Stack and Associates, 8; Unicorn Stock Photos/Robert W. Ginn, 9; Marilyn
"Angel" Wynn, 10, 27; Connie Toops, 12, 39; Cherokee Historical Association, 13; Photo
Network/Phyllis Picardi, 14, 16; Peter Turnley/Corbis, 15, 42; North Wind Picture Archive, 17, 23,
29; Hulton Getty/Archive Photos, 18, 19, 24, 30, 37; Stock Montage, 22, 26; Museum of New
Mexico, #154807, 25; FPG International, 28; The Newberry Library/Stock Montage, 31 (top);
Denver Public Library/Western History Collection, 31 (bottom), 38; Woolaroc Museum,
Bartlesville, Oklahoma, 32–33; Pat Anderson/Visuals Unlimited, 34; Bettmann/Corbis, 36, 40;
William Folsom, 41; John Elk III, 43.

Editors: E. Russell Primm, Emily J. Dolbear, and Alice K. Flanagan
Photo Researcher: Svetlana Zhurkina
Photo Selector: Catherine Neitge
Designer: Bradfordesign, Inc.

Library of Congress Cataloging-in-Publication Data
Press, Petra.
    The Cherokee / by Petra Press.
        p. cm. — (First reports)
    Includes bibliographical references and index.
    ISBN 0-7565-0079-6 (hardcover : lib. bdg.)
    1. Cherokee Indians—History—Juvenile literature. 2. Cherokee Indians—Social life and cus-
toms—Juvenile literature. [1. Cherokee Indians. 2. Indians of North America.] I. Title. II. Series.
E99.C5 C37 2001
975'.0049755—dc21   00-011066

Table of Contents

▲ A Cherokee chief wears a colorful headdress.

Who Are the Cherokee?

The Cherokee (pronounced CHER-uh-kee) Nation is the largest Native American tribe in the United States. Today, most Cherokee people live in northeastern Oklahoma. A smaller group lives on a **reservation**

▲ *The Cherokee once lived in what is now the southeastern United States.*

near Great Smoky Mountains National Park in North Carolina.

Once, the Cherokee were a powerful tribe. They lived and hunted in a large area of land. Today that land is part of the southeastern United States. They lived in what are now the states of Georgia, Tennessee, Alabama, North Carolina, and South Carolina.

The name Cherokee may have come from a Muskogean word meaning "people of a different speech." Or it may have come from a Choctaw word meaning "cave people."

Like many Native American tribes, Cherokee Indians call themselves "the real people" or the "**principal** people." In Cherokee, that word is *Ani-Yunwiya*.

The legend box reads:

Present-day Cherokee reservation

Map labels:

Minn. Wisconsin
Lake Michigan
Lake Huron
Lake Ontario
Michigan
New York
Iowa
Lake Erie
Illinois Indiana Ohio
Pennsylvania
UNITED STATES
Md.
W. Va.
Missouri
Ohio
Virginia
Kansas
Missouri
Kentucky
Arkansas
North Carolina
CHEROKEE
Tennessee
Oklahoma
Tahlequah (Present-day headquarters of Cherokee Nation of Oklahoma and United Keetowah Band)
Arkansas
South Carolina
Ala. Miss. Georgia
Texas
La.
ATLANTIC OCEAN
Mississippi
Florida
N
W E
S
Gulf of Mexico
0 100 200 miles
0 100 200 kilometers
MEXICO

▲ A map of past and present Cherokee lands

Villages and Clans

Thousands of years ago, the Cherokee lived in villages. They lived along the rivers of the southern Appalachian Mountains.

The Cherokee houses were made of tree logs covered with mud and grass. The roofs were made of tree bark. Families lived in these square or rectangular houses most of the year. During the winter, they moved into small, round houses.

▲ *The Cherokee lived along rivers.*

▲ *A Cherokee man in traditional dress*

Between thirty and sixty families lived in a village. They lived together in groups called **clans**.

A woman headed each clan. Each clan had a name. At one time, there were many clans. Now there are just seven—Wolf, Bird, Deer, Long Hair, Wild Potato, Twister, and Blue.

A large house stood in the center of each Cherokee village. The Cherokee held important meetings in this house. On an open field near this house, people held **ceremonies** and played ball.

▲ *A canoe hollowed out from a log*

Daily Life

Many foot trails and rivers connected Cherokee villages. People traveled on them when they visited, traded, and made war. They also used the trails when they hunted and gathered food.

The women gathered wild berries, nuts, and roots in the forests. They used honey and maple sap for making sugar. Men followed the trails when they hunted deer, bear, and elk. They also trapped fish in the cold mountain streams. They traveled on the water in wooden canoes.

Farming was an important part of Cherokee life. Each family had a field outside their village. There they grew corn, squash, sweet potatoes, tobacco, and beans.

In the fall, the whole village gathered the crops. The women stocked each house with food. Then they stored the rest in a community shed.

▲ *A Cherokee woman in North Carolina makes a basket.*

The Cherokee women made the meals. They made clothing from animal skins. They wove baskets out of plants and vines. Then they painted the bas-

kets with pretty designs. The women also made pots and jars from clay. They decorated them with designs too.

The Cherokee men carved pieces of wood. They made pipes and tools. Today, Cherokee craftspeople still make these beautiful objects.

◀ *A potter at the Oconaluftee Indian Village in North Carolina*

▲ A Cherokee dancer at a festival in Georgia

▲ *Healing a Cherokee woman*

The Cherokee were very religious. They believed that spirits lived in everything. They prayed often. They asked the spirits to help them in their daily lives. Then they thanked the spirits for their help.

People called priests performed ceremonies to talk to the spirits. The priests also held **festivals**. There were special ceremonies before hunting, going to war, or playing a ballgame.

15

▲ A colorful Cherokee dance costume

There were religious ceremonies for the sick and dying.

Music and dance were important in Cherokee religion. Sometimes people danced all night long. In some dances, people pretended to be animals such as the Bear or the Eagle.

The greatest festival of the year was the Green Corn Ceremony. It was held in July or August. At that time the corn was ready to be picked. People gave thanks for the good harvest of crops. Then they prayed for success in the new year. Today, the Cherokee still hold the Green Corn Ceremony.

Trading

▲ *Spanish explorers came to the Americas in the 1500s.*

In the 1500s, European explorers began to come to the Americas. The Spaniards came first.

In 1540, the Cherokee welcomed a group of explorers led by Hernando de Soto. The strangers

▲ *Hernando de Soto and his men*

had come on horseback. They were headed west.
Many years later, people from France and England
came to the area.

The French had come to trade. Some French men
lived among the Cherokee and started families. The
English settled in America too. They brought their
families with them. They were called **colonists**.

The Cherokee were happy to trade with the colonists. Cherokee hunters traded deerskins for iron pots, metal hoes, and guns. Iron pots were good for cooking. Metal hoes made farming easier. With guns, the Cherokee could kill more animals. That meant they had more skins to trade with the Europeans.

▲ *Native Americans traded animal skins for many different things.*

▲ *A Cherokee uses a traditional blowgun in North Carolina.*

Making War

Soon, hunting and making war were a big part of Cherokee life. These things became more important to the Cherokee than farming. Guns made war easier and the Cherokee were always at war with their neighbors. Meanwhile, Britain, France, and Spain were fighting one another for control of the land.

In 1715, the Cherokee made an agreement or a **treaty** with Britain. The Cherokee promised friendship with the Virginia colonists. They also gave the colonists some land.

In return, the colonists gave the Cherokee guns. It was the Cherokee's first of many treaties with the colonists.

The Cherokee were friends with the English colonists. But they got along better with the French. The French showed more respect for the Cherokee ways and beliefs.

In the French and Indian War, the Cherokee fought with the French against the British. This war began in 1754.

▲ *A battle during the French and Indian War*

▲ *Native Americans fought against the colonists.*

In 1763, Britain won the war against France. The British took land away from the Cherokee.

By 1775, many British colonists wanted to have their own government. So they went to war with Britain.

That war was called the American **Revolution**. The Cherokee fought on the side of Britain, but the colonists won.

On July 4, 1776, the United States of America was born. The United States took a lot of land away from the Cherokee. It took a large part of the states of South Carolina and Tennessee.

◄ *A Cherokee chief named Austenaco*

A "Civilized" Tribe

▲ *Chief Sequoyah worked out a written Cherokee alphabet.*

Over time, the Cherokee began to live like the American settlers. They lived in wooden houses and built towns. They gave up making war. They went back to farming.

During the 1820s, a Cherokee named Sequoyah worked out a written alphabet. Soon the Cherokee were printing their own newspaper.

The Cherokee built schools to teach their children

Cherokee Alphabet.

D o	R e	T i	Ꮜ o	O u	i v
S ga Ꝋ ka	F ge	y gi	A go	J gu	E gv
ꝍ ha	P he	Ꭿ hi	Ꮉ ho	Ꮁ hu	Ꮕ hv
W la	Ꮄ le	P li	G lo	M lu	Ꮑ lv
ꝑ ma	Ꮋ me	H mi	Ꮎ mo	y mu	
Ꮎ na Ꮏ hna G nah	Ꮐ ne	h ni	Z no	ꝗ nu	Ꮕ nv
Ꮖ qua	Ꮙ que	Ꮓ qui	V quo	Ꮚ quu	Ɛ quv
U sa Ꮝ s	4 se	b si	Ꮱ so	Ꮞ su	R sv
Ꮯ da W ta	S de Ꮦ te	Ꮧ di Ꮨ ti	V do	S du	Ꮫ dv
Ꮷ dla Ꮝ tla	L tle	C tli	Ꮬ tlo	Ꮭ tlu	P tlv
G tsa	V tse	Ꮅ tsi	K tso	J tsu	C tsv
G wa	Ꮃ wv	Ꮎ wi	Ꮼ wo	Ꮄ wu	6 wv
Ꮿ ya	B ye	Ꮙ yi	Ꮉ yo	G yu	B yv

▲ The Cherokee alphabet

▲ The Cherokee printed their own newspaper.

to read and write. They even set up their own government. It was like the U.S. government in some ways, but women had a larger role.

The Cherokee lived like the settlers in many ways. The settlers called them **"civilized."** The Cherokee were known as one of the "Five Civilized Tribes" of the southeastern United States. The other four were the Choctaw, the Creek, the Chickasaw, and the Seminole.

▲ *This painting shows, from the left, the "Five Civilized Tribes" of the Choctaw, Creek, Seminole, Chickasaw, and Cherokee.*

▲ *Gold was discovered in Georgia in 1828.*

By 1828, most Cherokee were living in what is now Georgia. That year, gold was discovered in the north Georgia mountains. Settlers began pouring in, hoping to find gold. They took the land and ordered the Cherokee out.

Two years later, the U.S. Congress passed a law. That law forced all Native Americans east of the Mississippi River to move to Oklahoma.

▲ *A Cherokee chief named Tah-chee refused to move to Oklahoma.*

▲ *Chief John Ross*

John Ross was the principal chief of the Cherokee Nation. He and other leaders tried to stop the U.S. government. But in the end, the U.S. government won.

In 1835, some of the Cherokee signed a treaty

▲ *The home of John Ross, near Chattanooga, Tennessee*

with the U.S. government. Most Cherokee were against signing the treaty. It gave away all the Cherokee lands. In return, the tribe received land in Oklahoma plus $5 million.

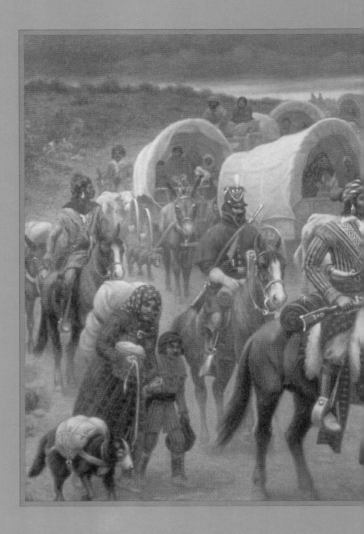

In 1838, U.S. troops rounded up about 17,000 Cherokee men, women, and children. They forced the Cherokee from their homes at gunpoint. They marched them to Oklahoma. Families could take only what they could carry. Few had warm clothing or food for the long trip.

▲ *The forced march of the Cherokee to Oklahoma was called "The Trail of Tears."*

It took more than six months to get to Oklahoma. Along the way, more than 4,000 Cherokee died. The forced march was called "The Trail of Tears."

▲ *Buffalo grazing on the Oklahoma prairie*

Life in Oklahoma

The Cherokee did their best to start a new life in Oklahoma. The U.S. government had given the tribe more than 8,000 square miles (21,000 square kilometers) of land. The Cherokee owned the land as a group. But each family could claim part of it for farming.

The first families who came to Oklahoma got the best land. They had come in the 1790s. The second group had arrived in 1837. The last group traveled on the Trail of Tears. By that time, the best land had been taken.

Soon people were arguing. They could not agree on what to do with the land.

In 1839, all the groups became one tribe. Then life got better for them. They called themselves the Cherokee Nation of Oklahoma. They set up a government.

By 1843, they had opened many public schools. They were also printing their own newspaper—the *Cherokee Advocate*. But, even then, the U.S. government would not leave the Cherokee alone.

▲ *The seal of the Cherokee Nation*

Three Cherokee Bands

▲ White settlers rushed to claim land in Oklahoma in 1893.

In 1887, the U.S. Congress passed a law. This law gave every Native American family in the United States 160 acres (65 hectares) of land to farm. The government sold the rest of the land to the settlers.

This law was not good for the Oklahoma Cherokee. It took away even more of their land.

In 1907, Oklahoma became a state. The new state was no longer only for Indians. More white people than Indians lived there. Many Cherokee began to mix with the white settlers.

Only a few Cherokee were able to live in the old ways. They kept the Cherokee language and traditions alive. But they were very poor.

▲ *Students outside a Cherokee school in Oklahoma in 1875*

▲ *A traditional Cherokee cabin in North Carolina*

The Eastern Band of Cherokee was poor too. These people had stayed behind in North Carolina when most Cherokee were forced to move to Oklahoma. Later, the U.S. government created a reservation for them.

▲ *An Oklahoma Cherokee woman in 1930*

In the United States today, there are three Cherokee groups. They are the Cherokee Nation of Oklahoma, the United Keetoowah Band in Oklahoma, and the Eastern Band in North Carolina.

Each has its own tribal government. This government runs the tribe's businesses. This government also takes care of the tribe's schools and social programs. Only the Eastern Band lives on a reservation, in North Carolina.

The Cherokee Today

▲ *A Cherokee man in traditional clothing*

Today, more than 300,000 Cherokee live in the United States. About 120,000 of them are in Oklahoma.

The Cherokee work in many different trades. Some are ranchers, farmers, doctors, lawyers, and teachers.

Others work in the arts. There are many famous Cherokee writers. Robert Conley, Marilou Awiakta, E. K. Caldwell, and Raven Hill are some Cherokee writers.

Women continue to be important in Cherokee life and politics. In 1987, Wilma Mankiller became the first modern woman to be principal chief of the Cherokee Nation. She was reelected in 1991. Chief Wilma Mankiller improved life for her people.

Since 1999, Chad Smith has been principal chief of the Cherokee Nation. He is doing a lot to save Cherokee culture.

▲ *Wilma Mankiller*

▲ *A man makes an arrowhead at the Cherokee Heritage Center.*

The tribe's greatest business is from visitors. Every year, people come to the Cherokee Heritage Center in Tahlequah, Oklahoma. It is one of America's best living museums. It shows what life was like in an ancient Cherokee village. Visitors also spend time in the tribe's bingo halls.

The Cherokee have learned how to live in the modern world. And they hold on to the beauty of their traditions.

Glossary

ceremonies—formal actions to mark important times

civilized—highly developed and well organized

clans—groups of related families

colonists—people who live in a newly settled area

festivals—holidays or celebrations

principal—first in importance

reservation—a large area of land set aside for Native Americans; in Canada reservations are called reserves

revolution—a war fought to change a government

treaty—an agreement between two governments

Did You Know?

- The grandmother of former U.S. president Bill Clinton was one-fourth Cherokee.

- Sequoyah was disabled. (*Sikwo-yi* means "pig's foot" in Cherokee.)

- The giant sequoia trees of California are named after Sequoyah.

- The Cherokee have a special dance called the Booger Dance. Dancers wear wooden masks to scare away "boogers." In the past, boogers were Europeans, ghosts, and other such monsters.

At a Glance

Tribal name: Cherokee

Past locations: Tennessee, North Carolina, South Carolina, Georgia, Alabama, Oklahoma

Present locations: Oklahoma, North Carolina

Traditional houses: In winter, small round houses with cone-shaped roofs; in summer, long rectangular houses with peaked roofs

Traditional clothing materials: Buckskin, feathers; later, cotton trade goods and ribbons

Traditional transportation: Wooden dugout canoes; later, horses

Traditional food: Corn, beans, squash, wild plants, fish, deer, bear, rabbit, turkey

Important Dates

1540   Spaniard Hernando de Soto marches through Cherokee lands looking for gold.

1715   The Cherokee sign first treaty with Britain and give up land.

1754–1763   The French and Indian War takes place.

1775   The Cherokee fight against American colonists in the American Revolution.

1820s   Sequoyah works out a written alphabet. The Cherokee publish a newspaper.

1838–1839   About 7,000 Cherokee are moved to Oklahoma and 4,000 Cherokee die during the Trail of Tears.

1839   Cherokee tribes form the Cherokee Nation.

1924   U.S. Congress passes a law making all Native Americans U.S. citizens.

1987   Wilma Mankiller is elected the first woman principal chief of the Cherokee Nation.

1999   Chad Smith is elected principal chief of the Cherokee Nation.

Want to Know More?

At the Library

Burgan, Michael. *The Trail of Tears*. Minneapolis: Compass Point Books, 2001.

Long, Cathryn J. *The Cherokee*. San Diego, Calif.: Lucent Books, Inc., 2000.

Lund, Bill. *The Cherokee Indians*. Mankato, Minn.: Bridgestone Books, 1997.

Sneve, Virginia Driving Hawk. *The Cherokees*. New York: Holiday House, 1996.

On the Web

The Cherokee Nation
http://www.cherokee.org
For the official tribal site for history and events

History of the Cherokee
http://pages.tca.net/martikw
For information about Cherokee history, images, maps, and links

Through the Mail

Sequoyah Birthplace Museum
P.O. Box 69
Vonore, TN 37885
To find out more about where this famous Cherokee was born

On the Road

The Cherokee Heritage Center
P.O. Box 515
Tahlequah, OK 74465
918/456-6007
(Three miles south of Tahlequah)
To visit the Cherokee National Museum

Index

About the Author

Petra Press is a freelance writer of young adult nonfiction, specializing in the diverse culture of the Americas. Her more than twenty books include histories of U.S. immigration, education, and settlement of the West, as well as portraits of numerous indigenous cultures. She lives in Milwaukee, Wisconsin, with her husband, David.